LINES ON THE UNDERGROUND

an anthology for Central Line travellers

Compiled by

DOROTHY MEADE & TATIANA WOLFF

Illustrated by Basil Cottle and Jonathan Newdick

CASSELL

Cassell Publishers Limited
Wellington House, 125 Strand
London WC2R 0BB

in association with the London Transport Museum

This edition published 1996
The material in this anthology was first published in
Lines on the Underground, 1994

British Library Cataloguing in Publication Data
A catalogue record for this book is available from the British Library

ISBN 0-304-34840-6

Distributed in Australia by
Capricorn Link (Australia) Pty Ltd
2/13 Carrington Road, Castle Hill, NSW 2154

Printed and bound in Great Britain by Hillman Printers Ltd

To Joe, Dora, Anna and Ben

*

And in memory of

M. M. W.

CENTRAL LINE

The Central Line holds the distinction of providing the longest possible train journey on the Underground without a change, from Epping to West Ruislip, a journey of 34.1 miles (54.9 km). With 51 stations spread along the 52 route miles of track it is also unusual in embracing one of the most heavily used sections of the Underground (Liverpool Street to Stratford) with the most lightly used (Epping to Ongar).

M.A.C. HORNE, *The Central Line*, 1987

West Ruislip

Oak from the woods [around Ruislip Common] was used in the 14th century for work on the Tower of London, in 1344 for Windsor Castle, and in 1346 and 1347 for Westminster Palace.

The London Encyclopaedia edited by Ben Weinreb
and Christopher Hibbert, 1983

Ruislip Gardens

Gaily into Ruislip Gardens
  Runs the red electric train,
With a thousand Ta's and Pardon's
  Daintily alights Elaine;
Hurries down the concrete station
With a frown of concentration,
Out into the outskirt's edges
Where a few surviving hedges
Keep alive our lost Elysium – rural Middlesex again.

JOHN BETJEMAN, 'Middlesex',
A Few Late Chrysanthemums, 1954

South Ruislip

The village [Ruislip] with its church, almshouses, and moated farm is now so closely surrounded on all sides by suburban developments that the small and fairly completely preserved nucleus of old building comes as a surprise from whatever direction it is approached. . . . The parish is richer in good farmhouses than any other in the county.

NIKOLAUS PEVSNER, *The Buildings of England: Middlesex,* 1951

Northolt

[Northolt] Airport was a base of Fighter Command and played a considerable part in the Battle of Britain. . . . On the afternoon of 29th September 1940, over 200 high explosive bombs fell in the Greenford area. . . . Churchill left here to inspect the crossing of the Rhine.

BRUCE STEVENSON, *Middlesex,* 1972

Greenford

. . . Parish of enormous hayfields
Perivale stood all alone,
And from Greenford scent of mayfields
Most enticingly was blown
Over market gardens tidy,
Taverns for the *bona fide,*
Cockney anglers, cockney shooters,
Murray Poshes, Lupin Pooters
Long in Kensal Green and Highgate silent under soot and stone.

JOHN BETJEMAN, 'Middlesex',
A Few Late Chrysanthemums, 1954

Perivale

She Peryvale perceiv'd prank'd up with wreaths of wheat,
'Why should not I be coy, and of my beauties nice,
Since this my goodly grain is held of greatest price?'*

* Peryvale, or Pure-vale, yieldeth the finest meal of England.

MICHAEL DRAYTON, *The Poly-olbion* Part I,
the Sixteenth Song, 1612

Hanger Lane

Turn to page 8 for North Acton

Hanger Vale Lane. An ancient way . . . there is widespread misunderstanding of the name. It is sometimes fondly supposed that the name has to do with hangmen or gibbets or . . . with aeroplane sheds. This kind of hanger is in fact a wood on a hillside, where the trees may be said to hang on by their roots.

R.N.G. ROWLAND, *The Street-names of Acton, Middlesex*, 1977

What is the matter with Hanger Lane?
I'm late and it's dark and it's pouring with rain,
The traffic is bumper to bumper again,
What *is* the matter with Hanger Lane?
Answer: Too many cars: take a train.

ANON.

Ealing Broadway

Change for District line

There was a young lady of Ealing
Who walked up and down on the ceiling;
She shouted: 'Oh heck!
I've broken my neck,
And it is a peculiar feeling.'

ANON., *Penguin Book of Limericks*
edited by E.O. Parrott, 1983

West Acton

To the west of Acton High Street . . . lived Bulwer Lytton, the novelist and statesman. Another prominent resident of Acton was Henry Fielding, the novelist.

HAROLD P. CLUNN, *The Face of London*, 1932

North Acton

Great was my joy with London at my feet –
All London mine, five shillings in my hand
And not expected back till after tea!
Great was our joy, Ronald Hughes Wright's and mine,
To travel by the Underground all day
Between the rush hours, so that very soon
There was no station north to Finsbury Park,
To Barking eastwards, Clapham Common south,
No temporary platform in the west
Among the Actons and the Ealings, where
We had not once alighted. Metroland
Beckoned us out to lanes in beechy Bucks –
Goldschmidt and Howland (in a wooden hut
Beside the station): 'Most attractive sites
Ripe for development'; Charrington's for coal;
And not far off the neo-Tudor shops.

JOHN BETJEMAN, *Summoned by Bells*, 1960

East Acton

The wells at Acton are seldom remembered . . . but they were uncommonly popular in their own time, even though to reach them from London involved a rather arduous ride. The Acton wells were 'rediscovered' in the reign of Queen Anne. . . . The spa achieved its greatest popularity during the reign of George III. The water was said with relish to be 'more powerfully cathartic than any other in the Kingdom of the same quality except that of Cheltenham', with the added inducement that the quantity of salts in each pound weight of the Acton water was forty-four grains. It must have been a powerful draught which attracted not only permanent residents to East Acton and Friar's Place, which adjoined the hamlet of East Acton, but thousands of visitors for the day from London.

CHRISTOPHER TRENT, *Greater London*, 1965

White City

The fourth Olympic Games were held in White City Stadium in 1908. The marathon distance of 26 miles had to be hastily adjusted to 26 miles and 385 yards to bring the finishing line directly in front of the Royal Box

Encyclopaedia of Britain edited by Bamber Gascoigne, 1993

Shepherd's Bush

Change for Hammersmith & City line

Shepherd's Bush Common. Triangular open space of 8 acres acquired by Act of Parliament 1871. It was formerly called Gagglegoose Green. Its present name is from the shepherd's practice of watching his sheep whilst lying in a thorn bush. The highwayman 'Sixteen String Jack' was finally captured here.

The London Encyclopaedia edited by Ben Weinreb
and Christopher Hibbert, 1983

I had been waiting now at Holland Park for a long time . . . the saving grace of the Central Line [was] the way that beyond Shepherd's Bush and Liverpool Street, it veered off at either end to outlying towns to the north. I stood for a minute or more with my toes over the platform's edge, looking down into the concrete gully where a whole family of nervous, sooty little mice shot back and forth as if themselves operated by electricity.

ALAN HOLLINGHURST, *The Swimming Pool Library*, 1988

Holland Park

[Holland] Park was once the grounds of Holland House, built in 1605–7 for Sir Walter Cope, whose daughter married the first Earl of Holland . . . [It] enjoyed a long heyday as a centre of political and literary society, for the third Earl's widow married Joseph Addison, the statesman and essayist, and, in 1768, the property passed to the Fox family. Charles James Fox spent his childhood here, and his nephew, the third Baron Holland, entertained brilliantly, numbering among his guests Talleyrand, Madame de Staël, Ugo Foscolo, Sir Walter Scott

Wordsworth, Thomas Moore, Fenimore Cooper, and his neighbour, the historian Lord Macaulay, who lived in Holly Lodge on Campden Hill.

ANN SAUNDERS, *The Art and Architecture of London*, 1984

Notting Hill Gate

Change for Circle and District lines

Nature puts on a disguise when she speaks to every man; to this man she put on the disguise of Notting Hill. Nature would mean to a poet born in the Cumberland hills, a stormy sky-line and sudden rocks. Nature would mean to a poet born in the Essex flats, a waste of splendid waters and splendid sunsets. So Nature meant to this man Wayne a line of violet roofs and lemon lamps, the chiaroscuro of the town.

G.K. CHESTERTON, *The Napoleon of Notting Hill*, 1904

The little cosmopolis of Notting Hill, its littered streets, its record exchanges, its international newsagents, late-night cinemas, late-night delis, was to hand. The elegant vacancy of the Park was admirably near; you could walk to the museums, to Knightsbridge even, and a little later in the year, to the Proms. And at the back, a block away, you were in Carnival country.

ALAN HOLLINGHURST, *The Swimming Pool Library*, 1988

I am an old and valuable customer of the Underground. It is by far the quickest and most efficient way of getting around central London, apart from walking, or possibly bicycling. The lines have their familiar idiosyncrasies, from the swift thrust of the Central to the heart of the City, to the perversity of the Northern, which sends six Edgwares when what you want is a High Barnet. The names of the stations are poetry, from Theydon Bois to Cockfosters. . . .

My daily journey to work from Notting Hill Gate to Tower Hill is the farthest you can go on the inner zone, making me feel smug that I am getting value for money. Over the years I have spent hundreds of pounds on the Underground. When it comes to getting around London, I am a mole.

PHILIP HOWARD, *The Times*

Queensway

Since Roman times London has sunk fifteen feet. Severe weather, combined with an abnormally high tide, threatened to engulf forty-five square miles of the centre, including most of Westminster, the City and London's valleys. John Stow's rivers would have surfaced once again. The Cabinet would have moved to Holborn, Parliament to Queensway, and the Ministry of Defence to Lacon House in Theobald's Road.

It never happened, and at a cost of £460m, a monster flood barrier . . . was built between 1975 and 1982 to protect the capital . . . it is the largest flood barrier in the world.

RICHARD TRENCH AND ELLIS HILLMAN,
London Under London, 1984, revised 1993

Lancaster Gate

In their house in Lancaster Gate or some country house which they took for the summer she [Lady Strachey] would sit at the head of the table around which her five sons and five daughters together with a certain number of their wives or husbands argued at the top of their Stracheyan voices with Stracheyan vehemence. Lady Strachey seemed entirely oblivious to or unaware of the terrific din. She delighted to tell one about the vanishing literary world in which she had been the intimate friend of Lord Lytton, Browning and Tennyson.

Leonard Woolf in *Coming to London* edited by John Lehmann, 1957

W. Gunn Gwennet, an illustrator of railway advertisements, complained of the poor quality and large number of advertisements in the Underground:– It is as though the guards on the Central London Railway shouted out: 'Next Station Pear's Soap, Beecham's Pills, Marblarch, Bovril.'

HUGH DOUGLAS, *The Underground Story*, 1963

Marble Arch

If you walk from Newgate Street . . . to Marble Arch, you will be crossing the same ground that for five hundred years, from the thirteenth century until 1783, the death cart took carrying condemned criminals from Newgate prison to their hanging at Tyburn: . . . the procession . . . began the steep ascent of Holborn Hill, which was sometimes called Heavy Hill. To 'ride up Heavy Hill' meant that a man's misbehaviour might one day lead him to Tyburn, while 'going west' meant that he was literally on the way there.

There were several other gallows in London and at first Tyburn was reserved for the upper classes, though not for long. The first hangings at Tyburn were a little to the west of the later site of the gallows, where the western tributary of the Tyburn river crossed what is now the Bayswater Road. The brook was lined with elm trees and the first recorded hanging was on one of these trees, when Roger de Mortimer, a lover of Edward II's wife, Queen Isabella, was dragged there on a hurdle, hanged, drawn and quartered and left there for several days. Later the place of execution was moved to the end of the Edgware Road, where today the Marble Arch stands.

MARY CATHCART BORER, *London Walks and Legends*, 1981

. . . they tell me that So-and-So, who does not write prefaces, is no charlatan. Well, I am. I first caught the ear of the British public on a cart in Hyde Park, to the blaring of brass bands, and this . . . because like all dramatists and mimes of genuine vocation, I am a natural-born mountebank.

GEORGE BERNARD SHAW, Preface to *Three Plays for Puritans*, 1901

Bond Street

Change for Jubilee line

What sauntering indifference is displayed in the steps of the well-dressed pedestrians, who at the accustomed moment commence their daily pilgrimage from the top of Bond-street to the end of Pall Mall! Some stop at the fruit-shops, and, careless of consequences, run up a bill for early strawberries, forced peaches, and pine-apple ices. . . . Some empty their purses in bidding for useless baubles at the splendid auction-rooms of Phillips and Christie. Some are attracted by the grotesque prints exhibited at the windows of the caricature-sellers . . . scarcely any can resist the varied temptations which shops of every possible kind hold out to the vanity or the wants of the passers by.

MARQUIS DE VERMOND, 1823, quoted by
D.J. Olsen in *The City as a Work of Art*, 1986

Oxford Circus

Change for Bakerloo and Victoria lines

The women who walk down Oxford Street
Have bird-like faces and brick-like feet;
Floppity flop go 'tens' and 'elevens'
Of Easiphit into D.H. Evans.
The women who walk down Oxford Street
Suffer a lot from nerves and heat,
But with Bovril, Tizer and Phospherine
They may all become what they might have been.
They gladly clatter with bag in hand
Out of the train from Metroland,
And gladly gape, when commerce calls,
At all the glory of plate-glass walls,
And gladly buy, till their bags are full,
'Milton' cleaner and 'Wolsey' wool,
'Shakespeare' cornflour, a 'Shelley' shirt,
'Brighto', 'Righto' and 'Moovyerdirt'.
Commerce pours on them gifts like rain;
Back in Metroland once again,
Wasn't it worth your weary feet –
The colourful bustle of Oxford Street?

JOHN BETJEMAN, 'Civilized Woman',
Uncollected Poems, 1982

Tottenham Court Road

Change for Northern line

LUNARDI'S SECOND VOYAGE

The most pompous, absurd, and ridiculous advertisements and paragraphs, had, for six weeks, announced to the publick, the glorious ascension of the Italian philosopher. Large bills, printed on pea green paper, for eight days, ornamented all the corners of the streets. . . . The GRAND BRITISH BALLOON, covered thick with paint, represented the arms of England, upon a ground of red and blue, imitating the St. George's flag.

Signor Lunardi had promised to elevate with him a young lady, without doubt, in emulation of Miss Simonet [of a rival's ascent]; but Miss Simonet weighed only eighty-three pounds, and Mr. Lunardi's lady two hundred and fifty. A scientifick gentleman, furnished with barometers, thermometers, hydrometers, sextants, quadrants, telescopes, time-pieces, etc. etc. etc. was to complete the philosophick cargo. The great citizen of Lucca was to *direct the machine,* the scientifick gentleman was to *take the altitudes,* and the lady of two hundred and a half, was to make *'interesting observations on the general appearances.'*

Each of these aeronauts had a separate department, and in case they met with the sea, the sea was to be crossed. These were the solemn engagements made to the publick; we now proceed to the result of them.

On Friday, to accomplish all these fair promises, at twenty minutes after one, the GRAND BRITISH BALLOON, plastered with four coats of colour, and appearing in the form of a flattened orange, elevated with great difficulty a gallery of 112 pounds, two or three bags of ballast, and Signor Lunardi *only.* The fat lady, who had swallowed a few spoonfuls of brandy, to recruit her *'heroism'*, and to dispose her *'liberal mind for the reflections she intended to make for the benefit of her fair country-*

women', finding herself left behind, made a national reproach to Lunardi for his neglect of her. . . .

It was fortunate, that the fat lady and the scientifick gentleman, did not accompany this new Icarus in his voyage, for having neglected, at the moment of his ascension, to open the appendices of his balloon, the dilatation produced by the heat of the sun, caused it to burst, at the distance of a mile from the place where he set out, and the pilot and the vessel descended, with considerable velocity, and landed at the skettle ground of the Adam and Eve publick-house, in Tottenham Court Road.

Morning Chronicle, 17 May 1785

Opinion was that Tottenham Court Road was the best pitch, the Central Line area. Tom didn't know that at that station you had to book your pitch in advance, add your name or the name of your band to the list under the No Smoking sign . . . busking was not what his grandmother and a lot of others seemed to think, just another kind of begging, but a real *musical* means of living, something you had to book and arrange like giving a concert in a concert hall. Unlike the noise made by the strummers who called it pop or country, his was serious music.

That day he committed himself to being a busker. He was a professional musician and the concourses of the Underground were his auditorium.

BARBARA VINE, *King Solomon's Carpet*, 1991

Holborn

Change for Piccadilly line

By the seventeenth century there was another stopping place on the way to the gallows, although only for the more gentlemanly prisoners. This was the Blue Boar [later the George and Blue Boar], on the south side of High Holborn, a stopping place on the way from Newgate prison to the gallows, where they were offered a glass of sherry. . . . Today, Number 285 High Holborn stands on the site.

MARY CATHCART BORER, *London Walks and Legends*, 1981

As clever *Tom Clinch*, while the Rabble was bawling,
Rode stately through Holbourn to die in his Calling;
He stopt at the *George* for a Bottle of Sack,
And promis'd to pay for it when he'd come back.

His Waistcoat and Stockings, and Breeches were white,
His Cap had a new Cherry Ribbon to ty't;
The Maids to the Doors and the Balconies ran,
And said, lack-a-day! he's a proper young Man.

JONATHAN SWIFT, 'Clever Tom Clinch Going to be Hanged. Written in the year 1726'

Near to the spot on which Snow Hill and Holborn meet, there opens, upon the right hand as you come out of the City, a narrow and dismal alley, leading to Saffron Hill. In the filthy shops are exposed for sale huge bunches of second-hand silk handkerchiefs, of all sizes and patterns; for here reside the traders who purchase them from pick pockets. Hundreds of these handkerchiefs hang dangling from pegs outside the windows or flaunting from the doorposts; and the shelves, within, are piled with them.

CHARLES DICKENS, *Oliver Twist*, 1837–8

Chancery Lane

LONDON. Michaelmas Term lately over, and the Lord Chancellor sitting in Lincoln's Inn Hall. Implacable November weather. . . . Fog everywhere. Fog up the river, where it flows among green aits and meadows; fog down the river, where it rolls defiled among the tiers of shipping, and the waterside pollutions of a great (and dirty) city. Fog on the Essex marshes, fog on the Kentish heights. Fog creeping into the cabooses of collier-brigs; fog lying out on the yards, and hovering in the rigging of great ships; fog drooping on the gunwales of barges and small boats. Fog in the eyes and throats of ancient Greenwich pensioners, wheezing by the firesides of their wards; fog in the stem and bowl of the afternoon pipe of the wrathful skipper, down in his close cabin; fog cruelly pinching the toes and fingers of his shivering little 'prentice boy on deck. Chance people on the bridges peeping over the parapets into a nether sky of fog, with fog all round them, as if they were up in a balloon, and hanging in the misty clouds. . . .

The raw afternoon is rawest, and the dense fog is densest, and the muddy streets are muddiest, near that leaden-headed old obstruction, appropriate ornament for the threshold of a leaden-headed old corporation: Temple Bar. And hard by Temple Bar, in Lincoln's Inn Hall, at the very heart of the fog, sits the Lord High Chancellor in his High Court of Chancery.

CHARLES DICKENS, *Bleak House*, 1852–3

St. Paul's

. . . the stones of St. Paul's flew like granados, ye mealting lead running downe the streetes in a streame, and the very pavements glowing with fiery rednesse, so as no horse nor man was able to tread on them.

JOHN EVELYN, *Diary, 4 September 1666*, on the Great Fire of London

. . . I had just extinguished my candle and lain down, when a deep, low, mighty tone swung through the night. At first I knew it not; but it was uttered twelve times, and at the twelfth colossal hum and trembling knell, I said: 'I lie in the shadow of St. Paul's.'

CHARLOTTE BRONTË, *Villette*, 1853

. . . St Paul's Cathedral is the finest building that ever I did see,
There's no building can surpass it in the city of Dundee . . .

WILLIAM MCGONAGALL (1825/30–1902),
'Descriptive Jottings of London', *Poetic Gems*, 1953

The Thames nocturne of blue and gold
Changed to a Harmony in grey:
A barge with ochre-coloured hay
Dropt from the wharf: and chill and cold
The yellow fog came creeping down
The bridges, till the houses' walls
Seemed changed to shadows and St. Paul's
Loomed like a bubble o'er the town. . . .

OSCAR WILDE, 'Impression du Matin',
Poems, 1881

Sir Christopher Wren
Said, 'I am going to dine with some men.
If anybody calls
Say I am designing St. Paul's.'

E. CLERIHEW BENTLEY,
Biography for Beginners, 1905

Initial adoption of the universal fare of 2d immediately attracted to the railway the friendly nickname of the 'Two-penny Tube'. The name was used by the Daily Mail *as early as 4 August 1900, and within a month had appeared in the New York press, where it was said that 'all London seems to be as pleased with its latest novelty as a child would be with a toy.' London newspapers showed real enthusiasm in recording that 'the crowds swayed and surged to get on to the trains . . .'*

. . . In the revival of the Gilbert and Sullivan comic opera 'Patience', the 'very delectable, highly respectable, three-penny bus young man' of the original 1881 performance, became the 'Twopenny Tube young man'.

CHARLES E. LEE, *The Central Line*, 1974

Bank

Change for Northern line and for escalator
to Monument for Circle and District lines

The first reference to tea by a Briton is in a letter dated June 27th, 1615. It was written by a Mr. Wickham, and is in the archives of the Old East India Company. It appeared in the September 2nd–9th, 1658 issue of *Commonwealth Mercury*, 'That excellent . . . by all physitians approved, China drink, called by the Chineans, tcha, by other nations, tay or tee, is sold at the Sultaness Head, a cophee house in Sweetings Rents by the Royal Exchange, London.'

In this same issue of the *Commonwealth Mercury* was a report of the death of Oliver Cromwell.

WILLIAM KENT, *London in the News*, 1954

The world's first electric tube of the completely modern type was the Central London, opened in 1900 – as a brass-plate in a subway at Bank Station still commemorates – by Albert Edward, Prince of Wales, K.G., in the last year before he succeeded to the throne. This was the famous 'Tuppeny Tube', so called from the uniform fare which was charged for any distance up to a total of its five miles run from the Bank to Shepherd's Bush.

MICHAEL HARRISON, *London Beneath the Pavement*, 1961

Liverpool Street

Change for Circle, Hammersmith & City and Metropolitan lines

Dear Mary,
Yes, it will be bliss
To go with you by train to Diss,
Your walking shoes upon your feet;
We'll meet, my sweet, at Liverpool Street.

JOHN BETJEMAN, letter to Lady Wilson, 'A Mind's Journey to Diss', *A Nip in the Air*, 1974

. . . The Central London from Bank to Wood Lane, extended to Liverpool Street in 1912, was the highest class line because it went by Bond Street to the City. It was also regarded as a sort of health resort, because it was ventilated by the Ozonair system, which was meant to smell like the sea, and certainly did smell of something. Air came out of grilles at the ends of huge aluminium pipes and sent a health-giving breeze down the platforms which caused the crinkly glass shades which hung over the white tiled stations to move slightly. . . .

JOHN BETJEMAN, 'Coffee, Port and Cigars on the Inner Circle', *The Times*, 24 May 1963

Bethnal Green

. . . and I by coach to Bednall green to Sir W. Riders to dinner – where a fine place, good lady, and their daughter Mrs. Middleton, a fine woman. A noble dinner and a fine merry walk with the ladies alone, after dinner in the garden, which is very pleasant. The greatest Quantity of Strawberrys I ever saw, and good. . . . This very house* was built by the blinde beggar of Bednall greene, so much talked of and sang in ballats (sic); but they say it was only some of the out-houses of it.

* Kirby Castle or Bethnal Green House. The blind beggar was reputed to be the son of Simon de Montfort.

SAMUEL PEPYS, *Diary, 26 June 1663*

It was a blind beggar, had long lost his sight,
He had a faire daughter of bewty most bright;
And many a gallant brave suiter had shee,
For none was so comely as pretty Bessee.

'The Beggar's Daughter of Bednall-Green', T. Percy's
Reliques of Ancient English Poetry, 1765

Rattling through the tunnel of the Central Line, I looked out furtively, affectionately, at my fellow passengers. Some had their eyes closed, some toyed with papers, some looked abstractedly upwards as if they were doing sums in their heads. Walls of black moss streamed past inches from the windows; looped cables, tool boxes. Each time the doors sighed open at a lighted station they let in a gust of subterranean wind. It tasted metallic, of burned carbon and newsprint – a warm, industrial mistral, as particular to the city as Big Ben or red buses. . . . Everyone aboard the carriage had mastered the trick of looking as if they were alone in an empty room. Everyone was travelling under sealed orders to a separate destination. In a fleeting conceit, I saw us all as members of the Underground, moving in secret through Occupied London, and for the first time on the trip, the city felt like home again.

JONATHAN RABAN, *Coasting*, 1986

Mile End

Change for District line

Being past Whitechappell and having left faire London . . . multitudes of Londoners left not me; but eyther to keepe a custome which many holde, that Mile-end is no walke without a recreation at Stratford Bow with Creame and Cakes, or else for love they beare toward me, or perhappes to make themselves merry.

Kemp's nine daies wonder. Performed in a daunce from London to Norwich . . . Written by himself to satisfie his friends, 1600

. . . we are, not absolutely in Whitechapel itself, but at the entrance of that peculiar and characteristic district, which I take to be bounded by Mile-end gate on the east, and by the establishment of Messrs. Moses and Son on the west.

First, Moses. Gas, splendour, wealth, boundless and immeasurable, at a glance. Countless stories of gorgeous show-rooms, laden to repletion with rich garments. Gas everywhere. Seven hundred burners, they whisper to me. The tailoring department; the haberdashery department; the hat, boots, shawl, outfitting, cutlery department. Hundreds of departments. Legions of 'our young men' in irreproachable coats, and neckcloths void of reproach. Corinthian columns, enriched cornices, sculptured panels, arabesque ceilings, massive chandeliers, soft carpets of choice patterns, luxury, elegance, the riches of a world, the merchandize of two, everything that anybody ever could want, from a tin shaving-pot to a Cashmere shawl. Astonishing cheapness – wonderful celerity – enchanting civility! Great is Moses of the Minories!

G.A. SALA, *Humorous Papers,* 1872

Stratford

Ther was also a Nonne, a Prioresse,
That of hir smylyng was ful symple and coy;
Her gretteste ooth was but by Seinte Loy;
And she was cleped madame Eglentyne.
Ful weel she soong the service dyvyne,
Entuned in hir nose ful semely;
And Frenssh she spak ful faire and fetisly,
After the scole of Stratford atte Bowe,
For Frenssh of Parys was to hire unknowe.

GEOFFREY CHAUCER, General Prologue to *The Canterbury Tales, c.* 1387

Leyton

It . . . was generally accepted that Leyton is the same as the ancient Roman station called Darolitum, though some antiquaries fix that at Romford. The discovery of coins, bricks, and pottery of Roman work here would seem to show that it was a place of some importance during the period of the Roman occupation.

E. WALFORD, *Greater London*, 1882–4

Leytonstone

Change for Epping branch

John Drinkwater (1882–1937), poet and dramatist, was born in Leytonstone.

HAINAULT BRANCH

Turn to page 27 for Snaresbrook

Wanstead

I went to see *Sir Josiah Childs* prodigious cost in planting walnut trees about his seate [Wanstead House], and making fish-ponds, many miles in circuit, in *Epping Forest*, in a barren spot, as oftentimes these suddainly monied men seate themselves.

JOHN EVELYN, *Diary, 16 March 1683*

[Wanstead House] . . . having added to the Advantage of its Situation innumerable Rows of Trees, planted in curious Order for Avenues and Vista's, all leading up to the Place where the old House stood as to a Centre. . . . The Green-House is an excellent Building fit to entertain a Prince, 'tis furnish'd with Stoves, and artificial Places for Heat from an Apartment, in which are a Bagnio, and other Conveniences, which render it both useful and pleasant; and these Gardens have been so much the just Admiration of the Publick. . . . The House is built since these Gardens have been finish'd: the Building is all of *Portland* Stone in the front, which makes it look extremely splendid and Magnificent at a Distance; it being the particular Property of that Stone, except in the Streets of London, where it is tainted and ting'd with the Smoke of the City, to grow Whiter and Whiter the longer it stands in the open Air.

DANIEL DEFOE, *A Tour thro' the Whole Island of Great Britain*, 1738

Redbridge

'What shall we see in Redbridge? There's surely a bridge,' he said,
'A bridge across the Roding, a bridge that's painted red.'
'My son,' the old man told him, 'things are rarely what they seem.
The old red bridge has long since gone, the Roding's an underground stream.

ANON.

Gants Hill

The most striking feature [of Gants Hill Station] occurs at the foot of the escalators, at platform level where the 'Moscow' concourse used for the Metropolitan at Kings Cross was again a major inspiration. . . . The work had been planned by Oliver Hill, and it earned him the Festival of Britain award for architectural merit in 1951.

LAURENCE MENEAR, *London's Underground Stations*, 1983

Newbury Park

A man went to Newbury Park
Expecting a bit of a lark.
'It's one of those places
I thought would have races –
I see I'm quite wide of the mark.'

JOHN GRIMSHAW, 1994

Barkingside

Barkingside is an altogether charming station. One can sit here on a misty day hearing nothing but birdsong and almost imagine that the peace will only be disturbed by the arrival of a steam train. Those illusions are shattered by the appearance of a standard tube train fresh from its journey under the centre of London.

LAURENCE MENEAR, *London's Underground Stations*, 1983

Fairlop

The Fairlop fair was founded by Daniel Day, who was born in Southwark in 1683 and was the owner of a small estate at Hainault. An eccentric extrovert, Day used to visit his estate on the first Friday in July for the purpose of collecting the rents from his tenants. He invariably took the opportunity provided by this occasion to entertain his friends, whom he regaled with beans and bacon under the spreading canopy of the Fairlop oak in Hainault Forest. This annual function developed into the Fairlop fair, and long before Day's death had ceased to be a private affair. The oak itself had a girth of thirty-six feet and was virtually destroyed by fire in June, 1805, the gutted trunk finally yielding to the elements when it was blown down by a gale in February 1820. . . . The timber from the old tree still survives, for from it was fashioned the pulpit of St. Pancras Church. As for Day himself, he died in 1767 and was buried in a coffin also made from a bough of the celebrated oak.

KENNETH NEALE, *Discovering Essex in London*, 1970

Hainault

With human bellow, bovine blare,
Glittering trumpery, gaudy ware,
The life of Romford market-square
Set all our pulses pounding:
The gypsy drover with his stick,
The huckster with his hoary trick,
The pork with fat six inches thick
And sausages abounding:

Stalls of apples, stacks of cake,
Piles of kippers, haddocks, hake,
Great slabs of toffee that men make,
Which urchins eye and pray for:
Divine abundance! glorious day!
We stayed as long as we could stay,
Then upped our loads and went our way
With all that we could pay for. . . .

Threading the silent, mist bedewed
And darkening thicks of Hainault Wood,
We reached that cottage, low and rude,
Which was so dear a dwelling;
By the black yew, solemn and still,
Under the brow of Crabtree Hill;
Ah dear it was, and ever will
Be dear beyond all telling.

Dry hornbeam twigs roared up in flame,
The kettle quivered to the same,
When home the weary parents came
The sausages were frying;
The tea was brewed, the toast was brown –
We chattered of our day in town;
Outside the leaves went whispering down,
And autumn owls were crying. . . .

RUTH PITTER, 'Romford Market',
Poems 1926–66

Grange Hill

. . . passing that part of the Great Forest which we now call Heinault Forest [near Grange Hill], came into that which is now the Great Road, a little on this side the Whalebone; a Place on the Road so called, because a Rib-bone of a great Whale, which was taken in the River of Thames the Year that Oliver Cromwel died, 1658, was fixed there for a Monument of that monstrous Creature, it being at first about eight and twenty Foot long.

DANIEL DEFOE, *A Tour thro' the Whole Island of Great Britain*, 1738

Chigwell

Chigwell, my dear fellow, is the greatest place in the world. Name your day for going. Such a delicious old inn opposite the churchyard – such a lovely ride, such beautiful forest scenery – such an out-of-the-way, rural, place – such a sexton! I say again, name your day.

CHARLES DICKENS, letter to John Forster, 25 March 1841

The day was named at once. . . . His promise was exceeded by our enjoyment; and his delight in the double recognition, of himself and of *Barnaby*, by the landlord of the nice old inn, far exceeded any pride he would have taken in what the world thinks the highest sort of honour.

JOHN FORSTER, *The Life of Charles Dickens*, 1872–4

Roding Valley

Ilford Bridge was the limit of commercial navigation on the Roding. . . . A considerable trade was done in timber, coal, gravel, cement and sand, but this declined sharply in the 1920s and the barge traffic ceased about 1930.

The London Encyclopaedia edited by Ben Weinreb
and Christopher Hibbert, 1983

EPPING BRANCH

It was a cold, dry, and dusty morning, and that the huntsmen of the east were all abroad by nine o'clock, trotting, fair and softly, down the road, on great nine-hand skyscrapers, nimble daisy-cutting nags, flowing-tailed chargers, and ponies no bigger than the learned one at Astley's. . . . Every gentleman was arrayed after his own particular taste, in blue, brown, or black – in dress-coats, long coats, short coats, frock coats, great coats, and no-coats; in drab-slacks, and slippers; – in gray tights, and black-spurred Wellingtons; in nankeen bomb-balloons; – in city-white cotton-cord unmentionables, with jockey toppers, and in Russian-drill down-belows, as a memento *to the late czar. The ladies all wore a goose-skin under-dress, in compliment to the north-easter.*

At that far-famed spot, the brow above Fairmead bottom, by twelve o'clock, there were not less than three thousand merry lieges then and there assembled . . . Fair dames 'in purple and in pall', reposed in vehicles. . . .

But where the deuce is the stag all this while? One o'clock, and no stag. TWO o'clock, and no stag! . . . Precisely at half-past two o'clock the stag-cart was seen coming over the hill by the Baldfaced Stag, and hundreds of horsemen and gig-men rushed gallantly forward to meet and escort it to the top of Fairmead bottom, amidst such whooping and hallooing, as made all the forest echo again. . . . For a moment, all was deep, silent, breathless anxiety; and the doors of the cart were thrown open, and out popped a strapping four-year-old red buck, fat as a porker with a chaplet of flowers round his neck, a girth of divers coloured ribbons, and a long pink and blue streamer depending from the summit of his branching horns. . . .

Presently, he caught a glimpse of the hounds and the huntsmen, waiting for him at the bottom, and in an instant off he bounded. . . . Then might be seen, gentlemen running about without their horses, and horses galloping about without their gentlemen; and hats out of number brushed off their owners' heads by the rude branches of the trees; and everybody asking which way the stag was gone and nobody knowing anything about him; and ladies beseeching gentlemen not to be too venturesome; and gentlemen gasping for breath at the thoughts of what they were determined to venture; and myriads of people on foot running hither and thither in search of little eminences to look from, and yet nothing at all to be seen, though more than enough to be heard; for every man, and every woman too, made as loud a noise as possible. Meanwhile the stag followed by the keepers and about six couple of hounds, took away through the covers towards Woodford. Finding himself too near the haunts of his enemy, man, he there turned back, sweeping down the bottom for a mile or two, and away up the enclosures towards Chingford; where he was caught nobody knows how, for everybody returned to town, except those who stopped to regale afresh, and recount the glorious perils of the day. Thus ended the Easter Hunt *of 1826.*

'SIMON YOUNGBUCK', *Morning Herald,* Easter Monday, 1826, describing the Epping Hunt, quoted in William Hone, *The Everyday Book,* 1830

Snaresbrook

[Snaresbrook] has retained its identity largely because in 1856 the Great Eastern Railway gave that name to its new station at the bottom of Wanstead High Street. The earlier focal point had been the Spread Eagle coaching inn on the Woodford Road. . . . Now the Eagle, it still retains something of its former elegance.

The London Encyclopaedia edited by Ben Weinreb and Christopher Hibbert, 1983

South Woodford

We have all been through much together, and I am honoured to have represented you in Parliament [for Wanstead and Woodford] for so long. You have all shown a kindness and a support to my wife and myself through the years of war and peace that have been a joy, a comfort and a source of strength. We are both very proud to be Freemen of this great Borough. Long may it prosper in peace and happiness.

SIR WINSTON CHURCHILL to his constituents on the occasion of the Borough's Silver Jubilee, September 1962

Woodford

Change for Hainault branch

Turn to page 26 for Roding Valley

About the year 1629, and the 34th of his Age, Mr. *Herbert* was seized with a sharp *Quotidian Ague*, and thought to remove it by the change of Air; to which end, he went to *Woodford* in Essex, but thither more chiefly, to enjoy the company of his beloved Brother, Sir *Henry Herbert*, and other Friends then of that Family. In his House he remain'd about Twelve Months and there became his own Physitian, and cur'd himself of his Ague, by forbearing Drink, and not eating any Meat, no not Mutton, nor a Hen, or Pidgeon, unless they were salted.

IZAAK WALTON, *The Life of Mr George Herbert*, 1670

Buckhurst Hill

I love the Forest and its airy bounds,
Where friendly Campbell takes his daily rounds;
I love the breakneck hills, that headlong go,
And leave me high, and half the world below,
I love to see the Beech Hill mounting high,
The brooks without a bridge, and nearly dry,
There's Bucket's Hill, a place of furze and clouds,
Which evening in a golden blaze enshrouds.

JOHN CLARE, 'A Walk in the Forest' from poems written at High Beech, Epping, 1837–41

Loughton

The parishers of Loughton were given the right by Queen Elizabeth I to lop wood from trees seven feet from the ground (the lower branches being left for deer to feed on) from the 11th November till 23rd April for winter fuel.

To retain this right they had to lop a bough before midnight on 11th November – failing to do so would lose them their lopping rights for ever.

On the 11th of November 1859 an agent for the Lord of the Manor named Richardson (also called The Bulldog) ordered a dinner at the King's Head Loughton and invited all the loppers. The wine flowed freely and all got drunk, all except old Thomas Willingale who had been warned by a lawyer, Mr. Buxton, not to touch any drink. Tom took his axe with him, went to Staples Road, lopped the bough and returned to the King's Head on the stroke of midnight, thereby saving the lopping rights.

For 16 years old Tom defied the Lord of the Manor and lopped wood, which he sold the parishers, from his woodyard in Whitaker Way, Baldwyns Hill. . . . Willingale Road and School are named after old Tom.

WALTER BULLEN, great-grandson of Thomas Willingale, 'The condensed history of Epping Forest & the Willingale Family' quoted in Barbara Pratt, *The Loppers of Loughton*, 1981

Debden

Debden, variously recorded in bygone days, in different chronicles, as Depden, Deepden, Depdon, Dependon, Dependana, Dependin, from Saxon words all of which mean 'a valley'.

W.G. RAMSEY with R.L. FOWKES, *Epping Forest Then and Now*, 1986

In the heady days of the Great Eastern Railway steam trains, and later LNER, the station was called Chigwell Lane. Surrounded by farmland and attracting remarkably few passengers, it was known as 'Paraffin Junction' because of old fashioned oil lamps when other stations along the line boasted electric light. It was serviced by two kindly porters who worked in shifts, one of whom whistled as he strode the platforms to attend the lamps and announce the up trains in a sing-song as 'LIVERpool Street train' or 'FENchurch Street line', usually for the benefit of three passengers already ensconced on board.*

JOHN SLEAP, Childhood Reminiscences, 1994

**It is still the least used station on the underground system.*

Theydon Bois

I was born and bred in its neighbourhood, and when I was a boy and young man I knew it yard by yard from Wanstead to the Theydons and from Hale End to the Fairlop Oak. . . . The special character of it was derived from the fact that by far the greater part was a wood of hornbeams, a tree not common save in Essex and Herts. It was certainly the biggest hornbeam wood in these islands and I suppose in the world. . . . It has a peculiar charm not to be found in any other forest.

WILLIAM MORRIS quoted by J.W. Mackail in
The Life of William Morris, 1899

There was a tube map on the station platform just as there had always been on stations. Victor didn't bother to look at it because the indicator informed him that the next train due would be going to Epping. It wasn't quite at the extreme other end of the Central Line but almost. A small subsidiary line went on to North Weald and Ongar during the rush hours. He stood on the platform with a return ticket for Epping in his pocket, waiting for the train that would go no further than Epping. . . . The journey was long and slow, for the line soon entered the tunnel, and would not emerge again till the eastern edge of London. Victor had bought *Ellery Queen's Mystery Magazine* and *Private Eye* to read. . . . The train finally emerged from the tunnel after Leyton. Victor had never been this far along the line before. This was deepest suburbia, the view being of the backs of houses with long gardens full of grass and flowers and pear trees in bloom running down to the track. Four more stations of this sort of thing and then, after Buckhurst Hill, a burst of countryside, part of the Green Belt encircling London.

Loughton, Debden, and what seemed to be an enormous estate of council houses with industrial areas. The train came out into more or less unspoiled country again, slowed and drew to a stop. The station was Theydon Bois.

RUTH RENDELL, *Live Flesh*, 1986

Epping

So we went to our Inn, and after eating of something, and kissed the daughter of the house, she being very pretty, we took leave; and so that night, the road pretty good but the weather rainy, to Eping. Where we sat and played a game at draughts; and after supper and some merry talk with a plain bold maid of the house, we went to bed.

Up in the morning. . . . Then to horse and for London through the Forrest, where we found the way good. . . .

SAMUEL PEPYS, *Diary, 27–8 February 1660*

Oh, take me from the busy crowd,
  I cannot bear the noise.
For Nature's voice is never loud;
  I seek for quiet joys. . . .

And quiet Epping pleases well,
  Where Nature's love delays;
I joy to see the quiet place,
  And wait for better days.

JOHN CLARE, 'Sighing for Retirement' from poems written at High Beech, Epping, 1837–41

ACKNOWLEDGEMENTS

We would like to thank our families and friends who have helped us over the years during the preparation of this book, especially Sandy Marriage, Robin Ollington, Bryan Rooney, Suzanne St Albans, Anthony Sampson, Kathleen Tillotson, Malcolm Holmes of the Camden Local History Library and the staff of the North Reading Room, British Library.

The compilers and publishers gratefully acknowledge permission to reproduce the following copyright material in this book:

John Betjeman: 'Middlesex' (*A Few Late Chrysanthemums* 1954) from *Collected Poems*, © John Betjeman 1958. 'A Mind's Journey to Diss' from *A Nip in the Air*, © John Betjeman 1974. *Summoned by Bells*,© John Betjeman 1960. 'Civilized Woman' from *Uncollected Poems*, © John Betjeman 1982. Reprinted by permission of John Murray.

Mary Cathcart Borer: *London Walks and Legends*, © Mary Cathcart Borer 1981. Reprinted by permission of Mary Cathcart Borer.

Bamber Gascoigne: *Encyclopaedia of Britain*, © Bamber Gascoigne 1993. Reprinted by permission of Macmillan.

Alan Hollinghurst: *The Swimming Pool Library*, © Alan Hollinghurst 1988. Reprinted by permission of Chatto & Windus.

Philip Howard: 'Wapping' and 'Philip Howard looks at London' from *The Times*, © Times Newspapers. Reprinted by permission of Times Newspapers.

Nikolaus Pevsner: *The Buildings of England: Middlesex*, © Nikolaus Pevsner 1951. Reprinted by permission of Penguin Books.

Jonathan Raban: *Coasting*, © Jonathan Raban 1986. Reprinted by permission of HarperCollins.

W.G. Ramsey and R.L. Fowkes: *Epping Forest Then and Now*, © W.G. Ramsey and R.L. Fowkes 1986. Reprinted by permission of Battle of Britain Prints International.

Ann Saunders: *The Art and Architecture of London*, © Ann Saunders 1984. Reprinted by permission of Phaidon Press.

Bruce Stevenson: *Middlesex*, © Bruce Stevenson 1972. Reprinted by permission of B.T. Batsford.

Richard Trench and Ellis Hillman: *London Under London*, © Richard Trench and Ellis Hillman 1984, 1993. Reprinted by permission of John Murray.

Barbara Vine : *King Solomon's Carpet*, © Kingsmarkham Enterprises Ltd 1991. Reprinted by permission of Penguin Books.

Ben Weinreb and Christopher Hibbert: *The London Encyclopaedia*, © Ben Weinreb and Christopher Hibbert 1983. Reprinted by permission of Macmillan London.

The publishers have made every effort to contact copyright holders where they can be found. The publishers will be happy to include any missing copyright acknowledgements in future editions.